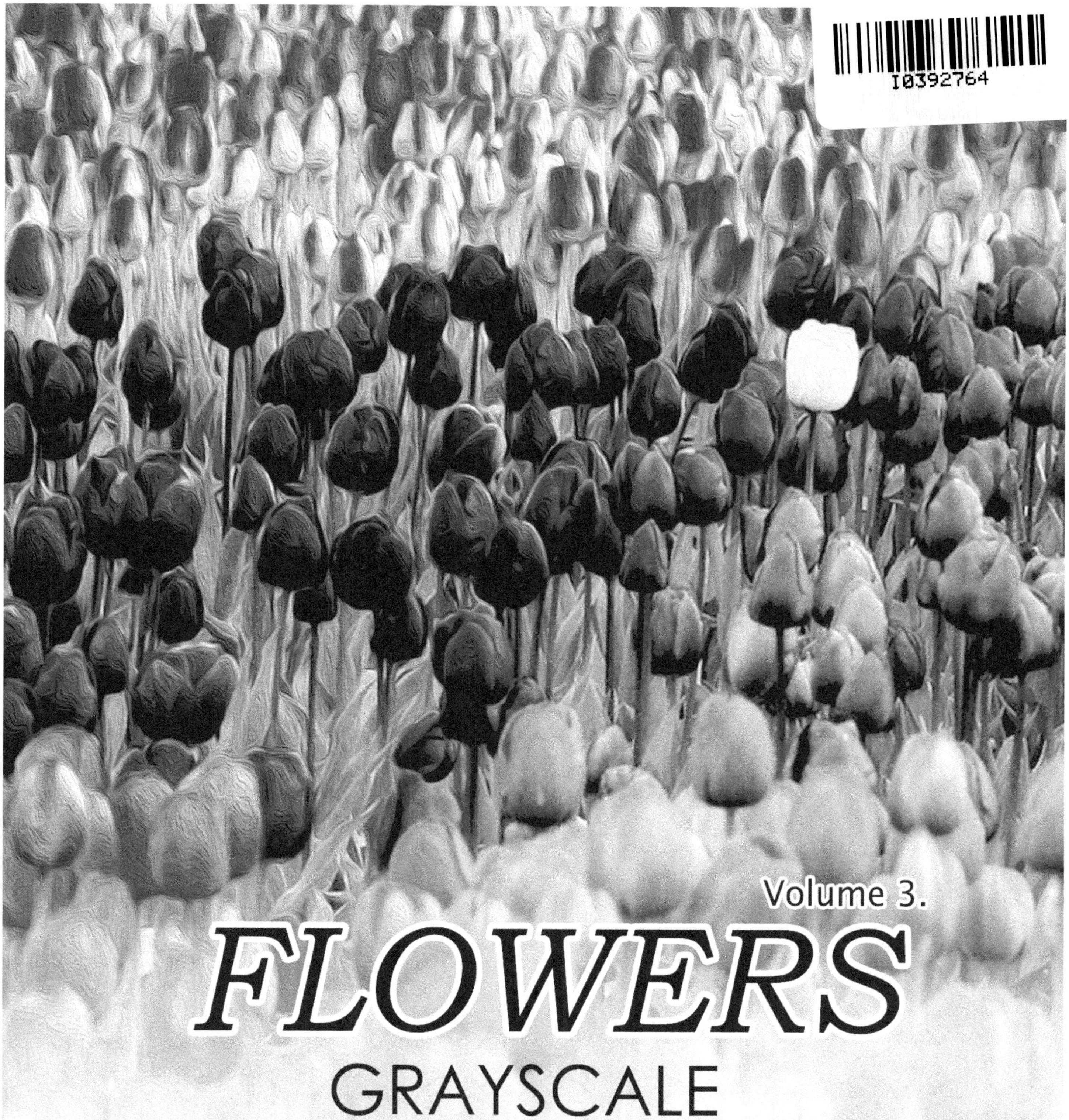

Volume 3.

FLOWERS

GRAYSCALE LANDSCAPE

COLORING BOOKS

COLOR TEST PAGE

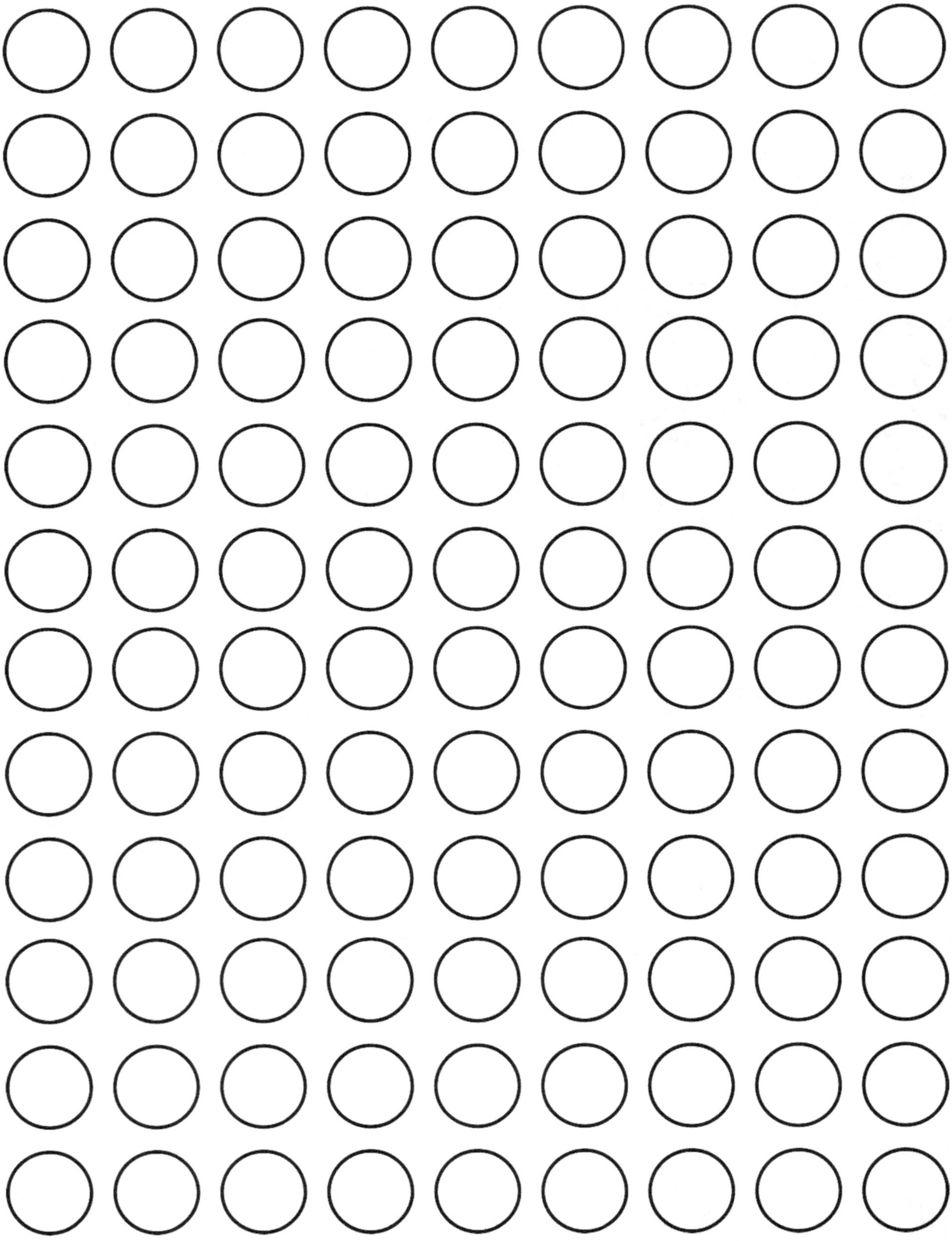

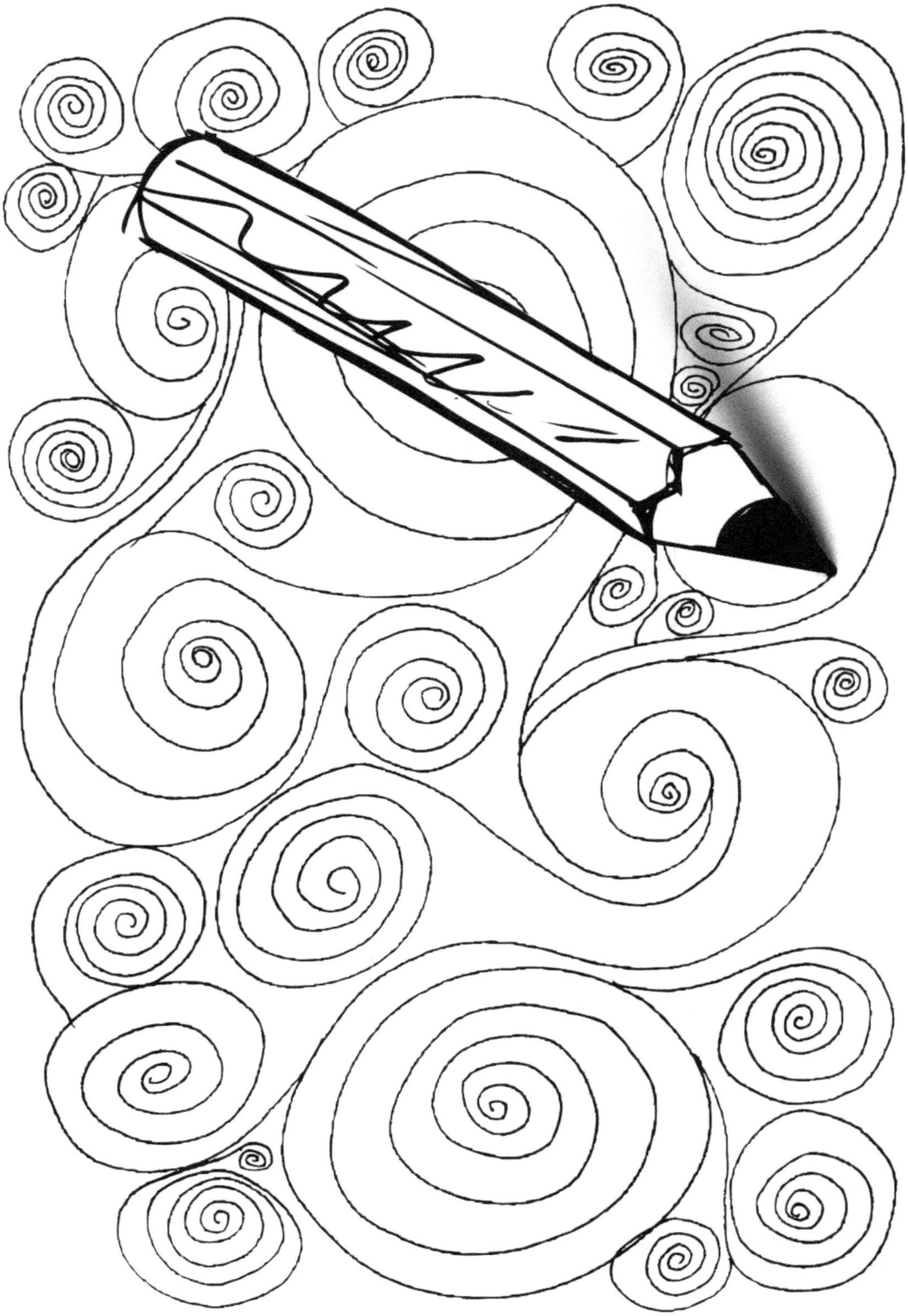

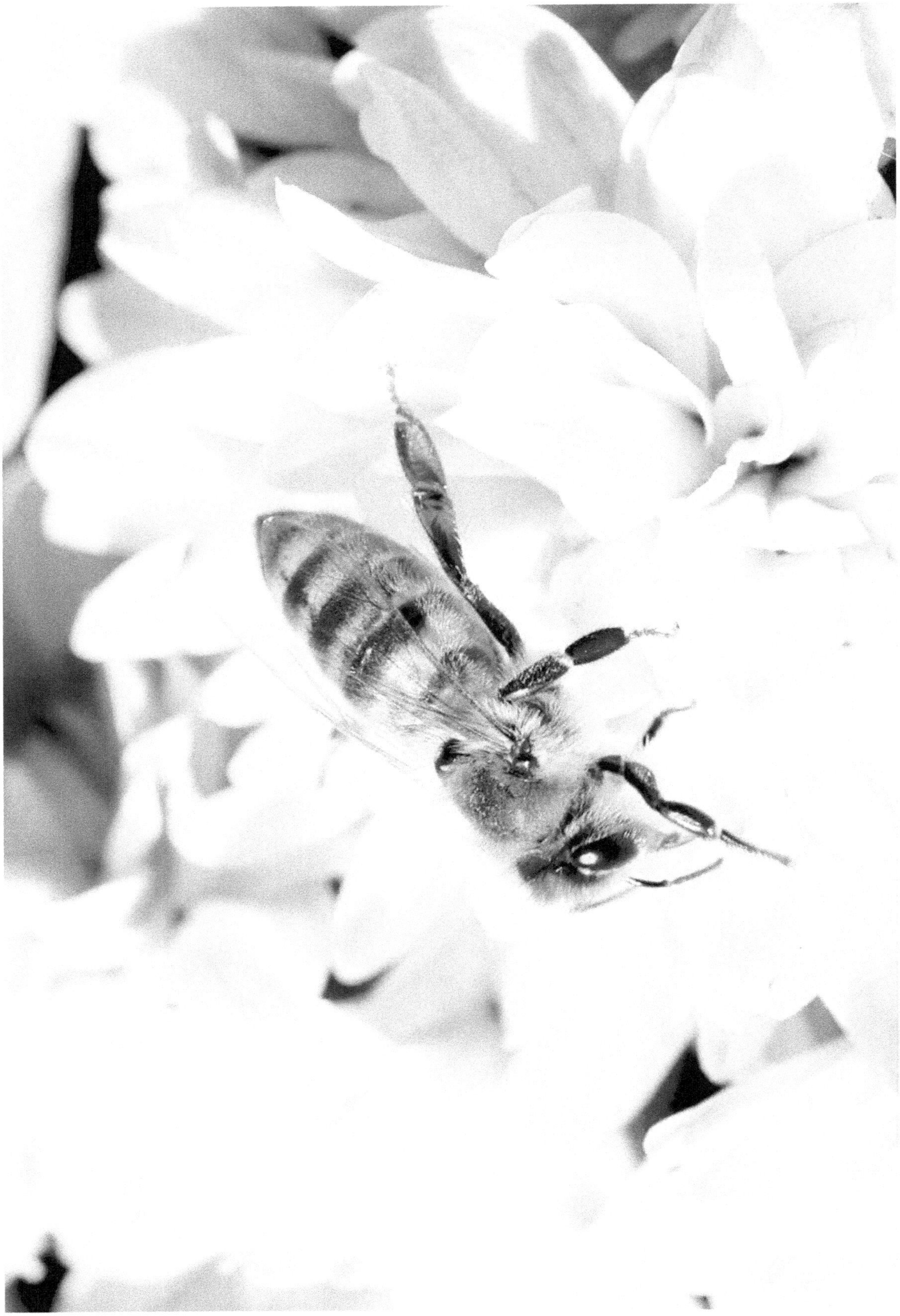

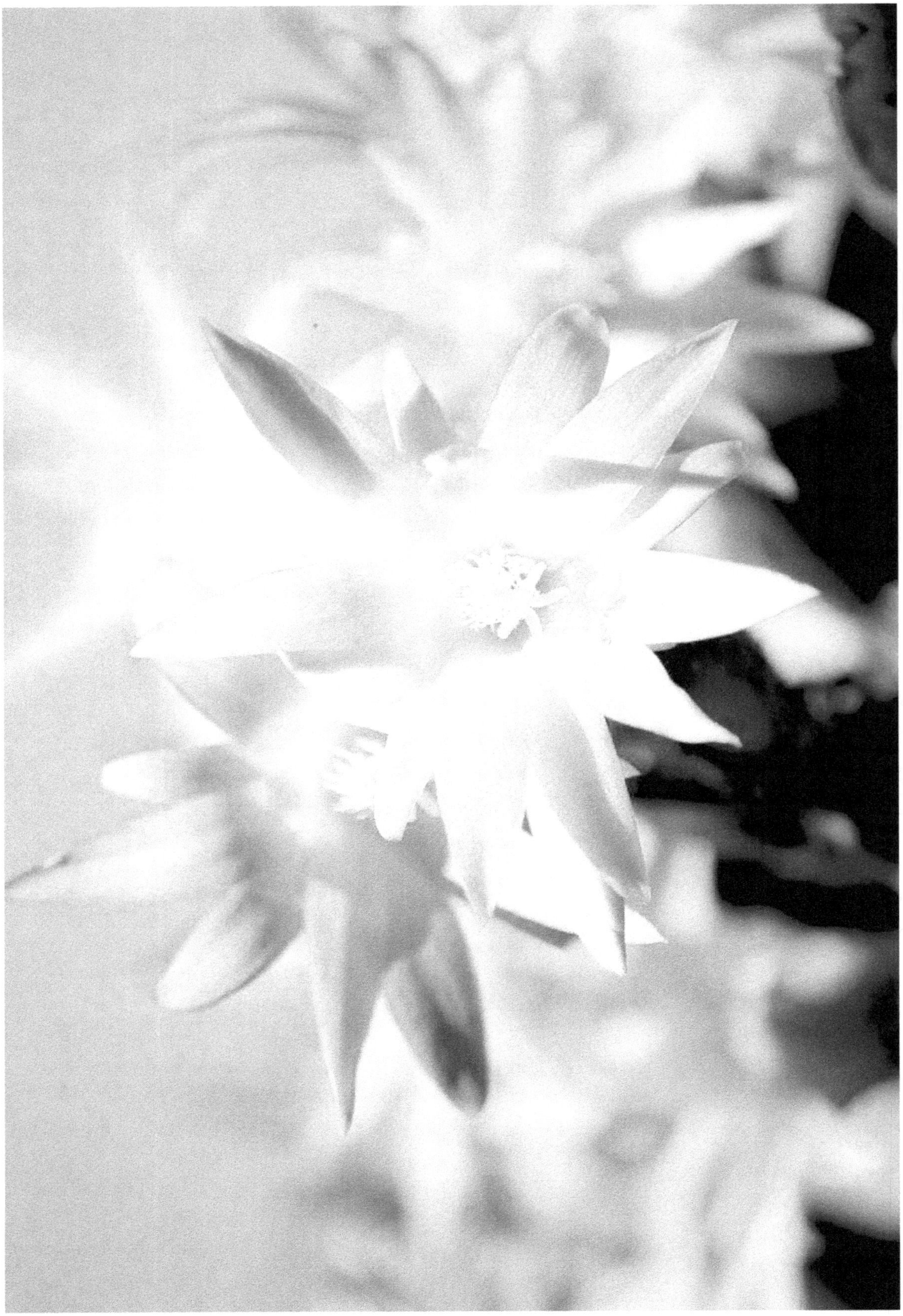

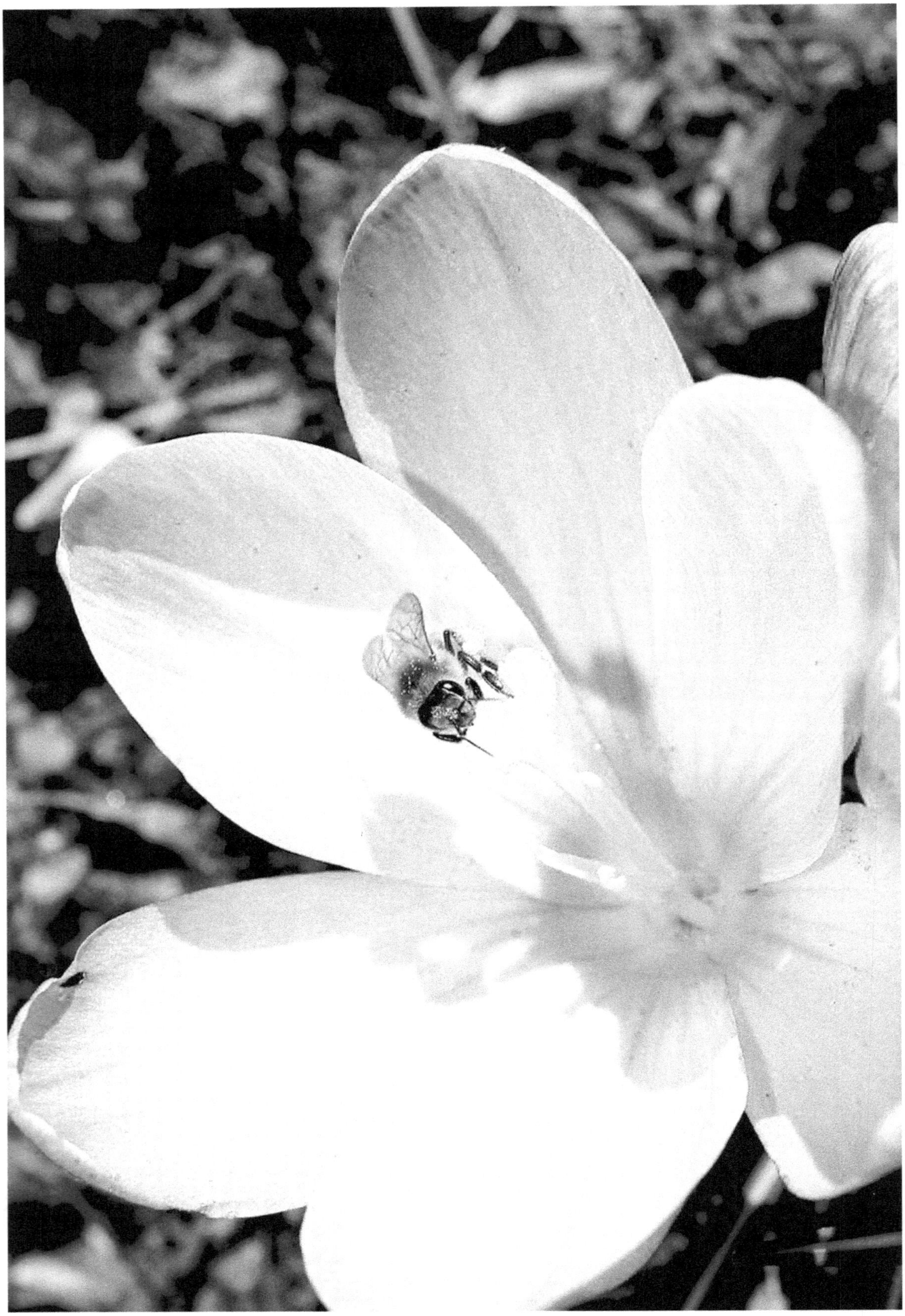

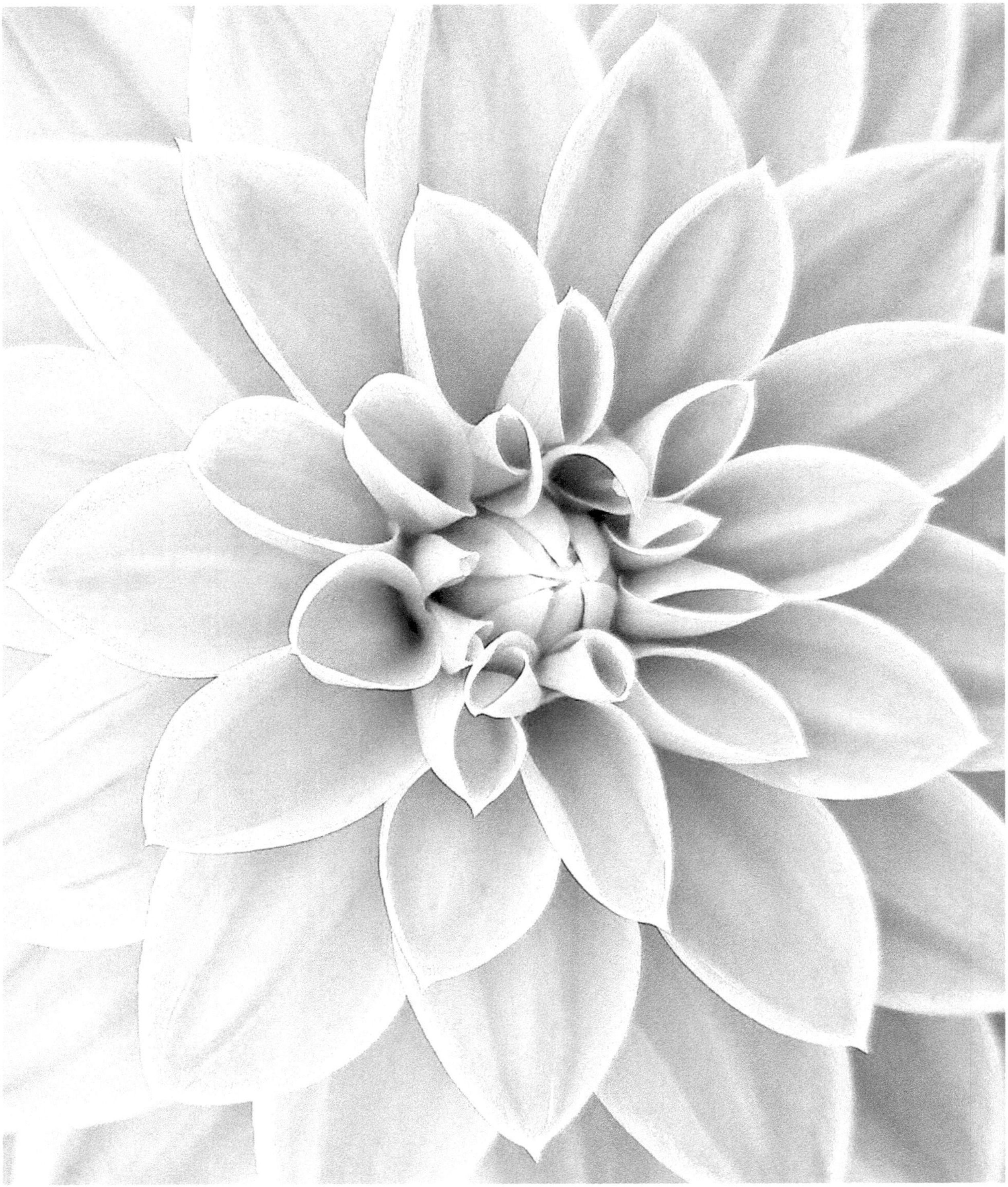

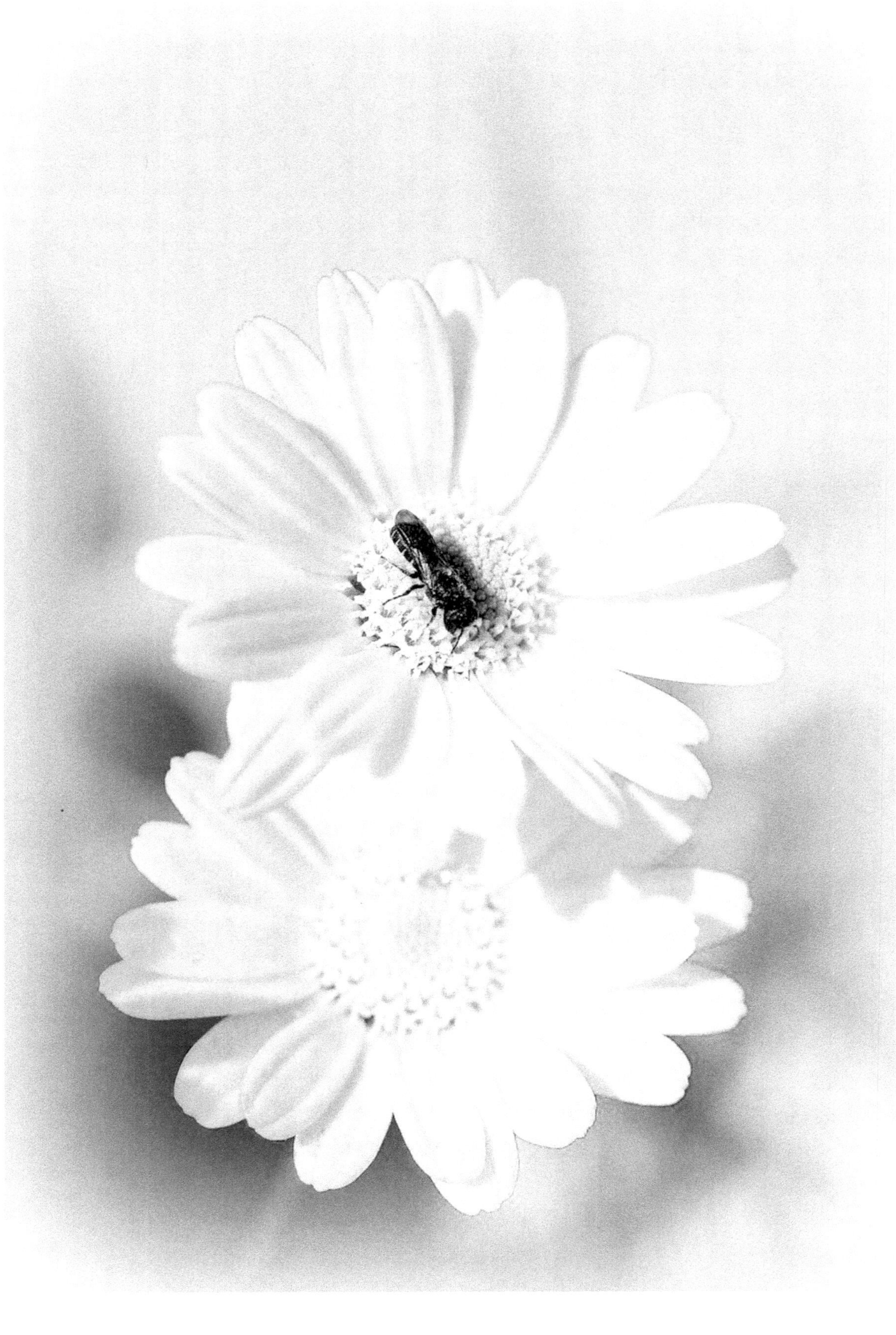

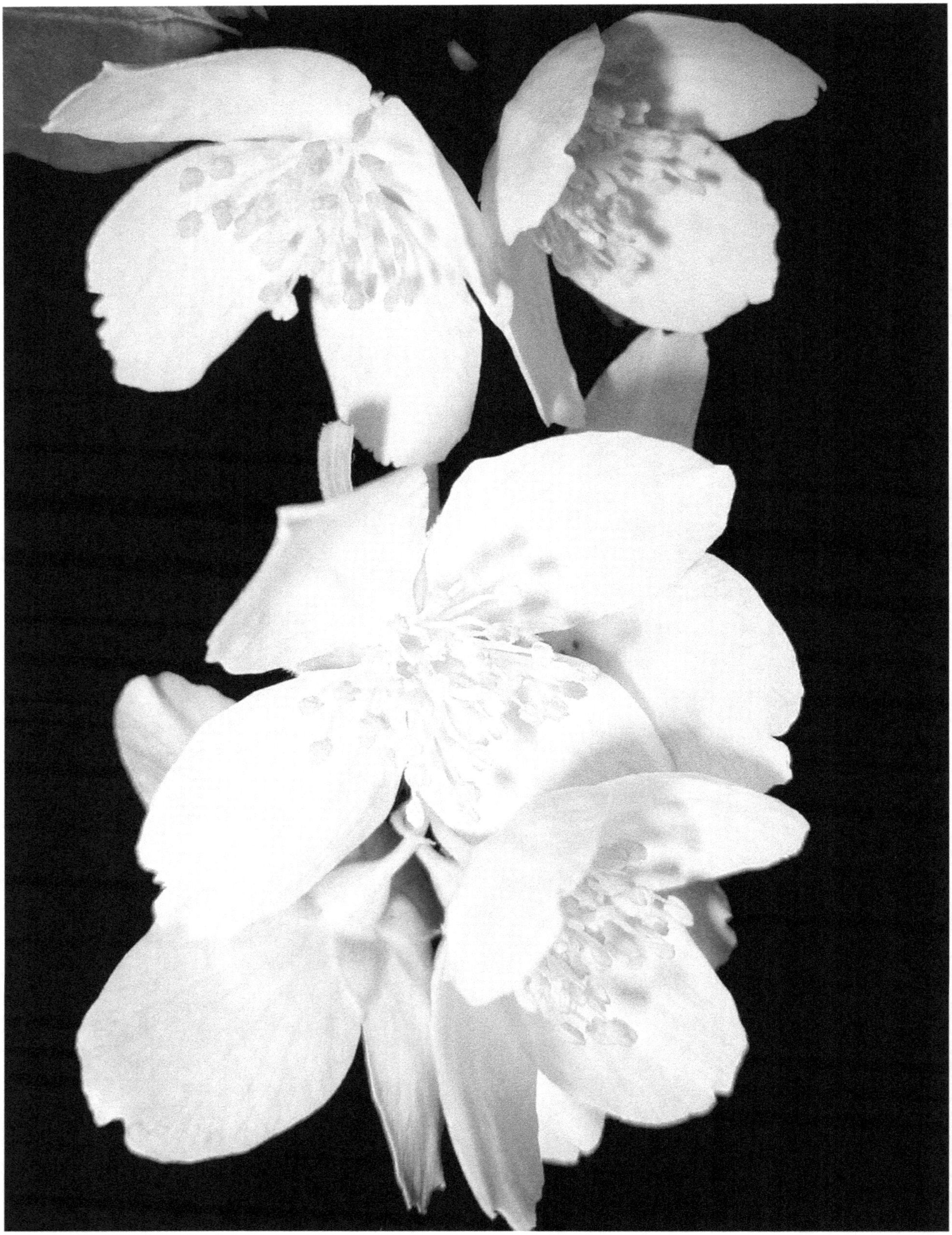

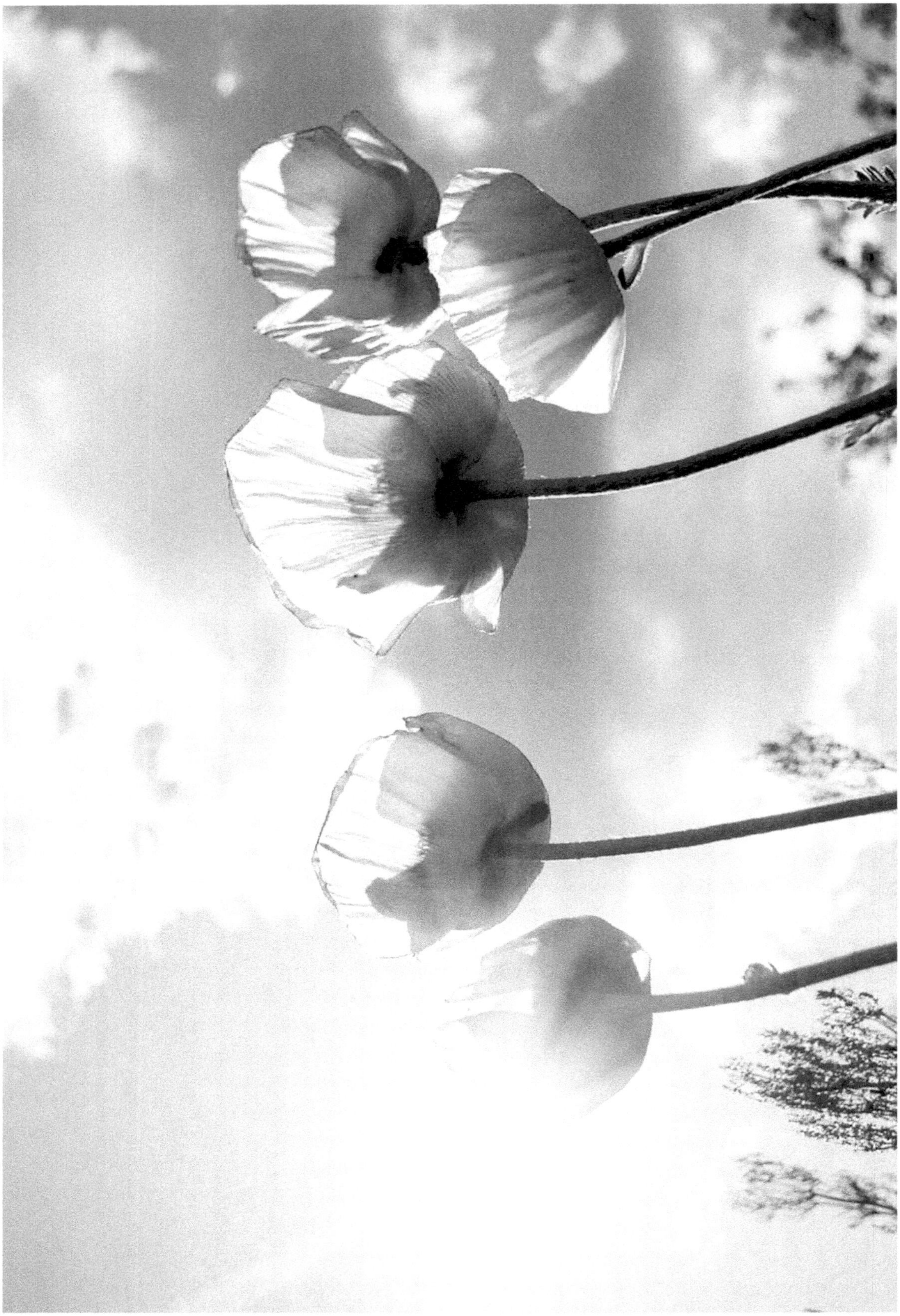

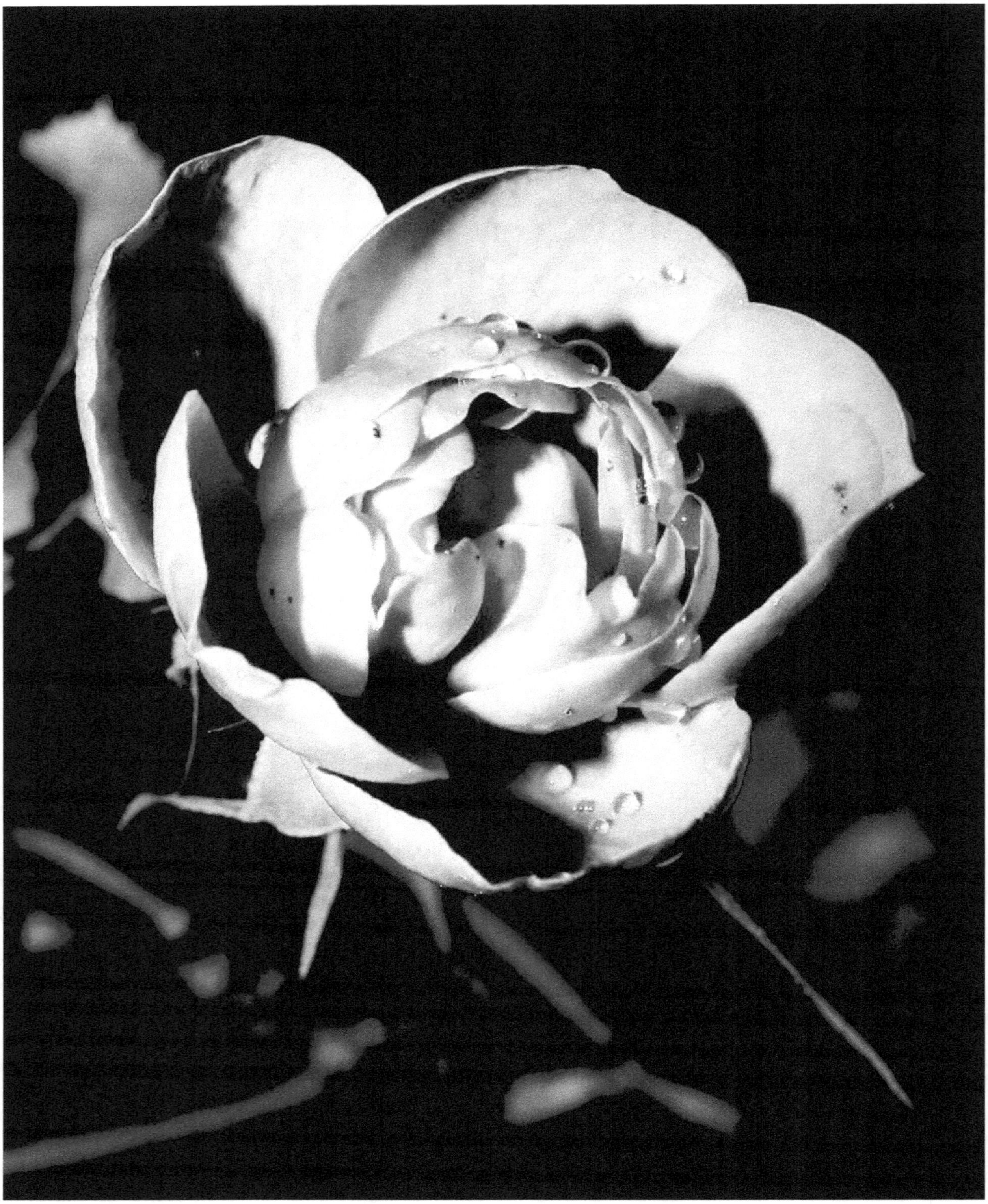

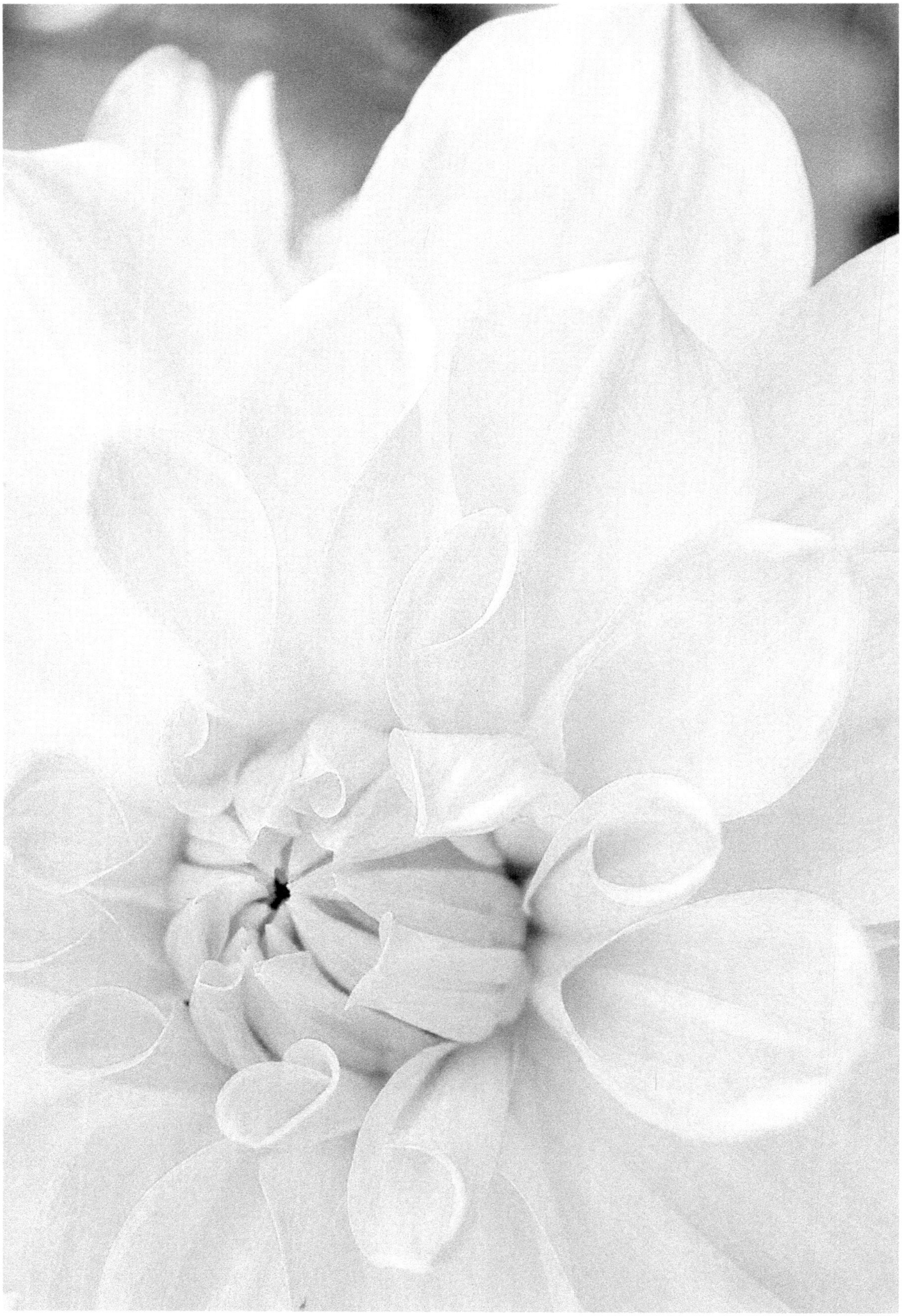

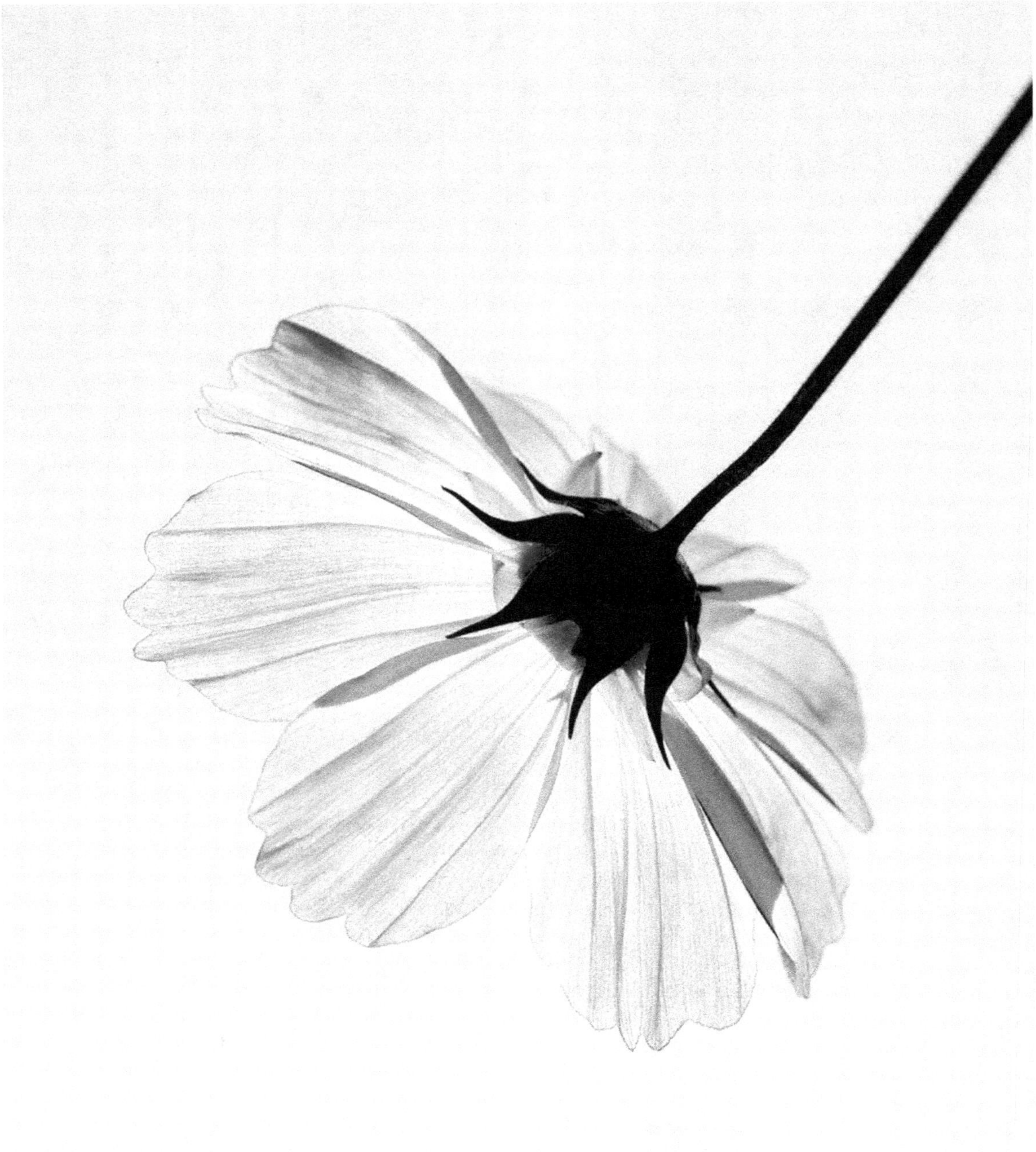

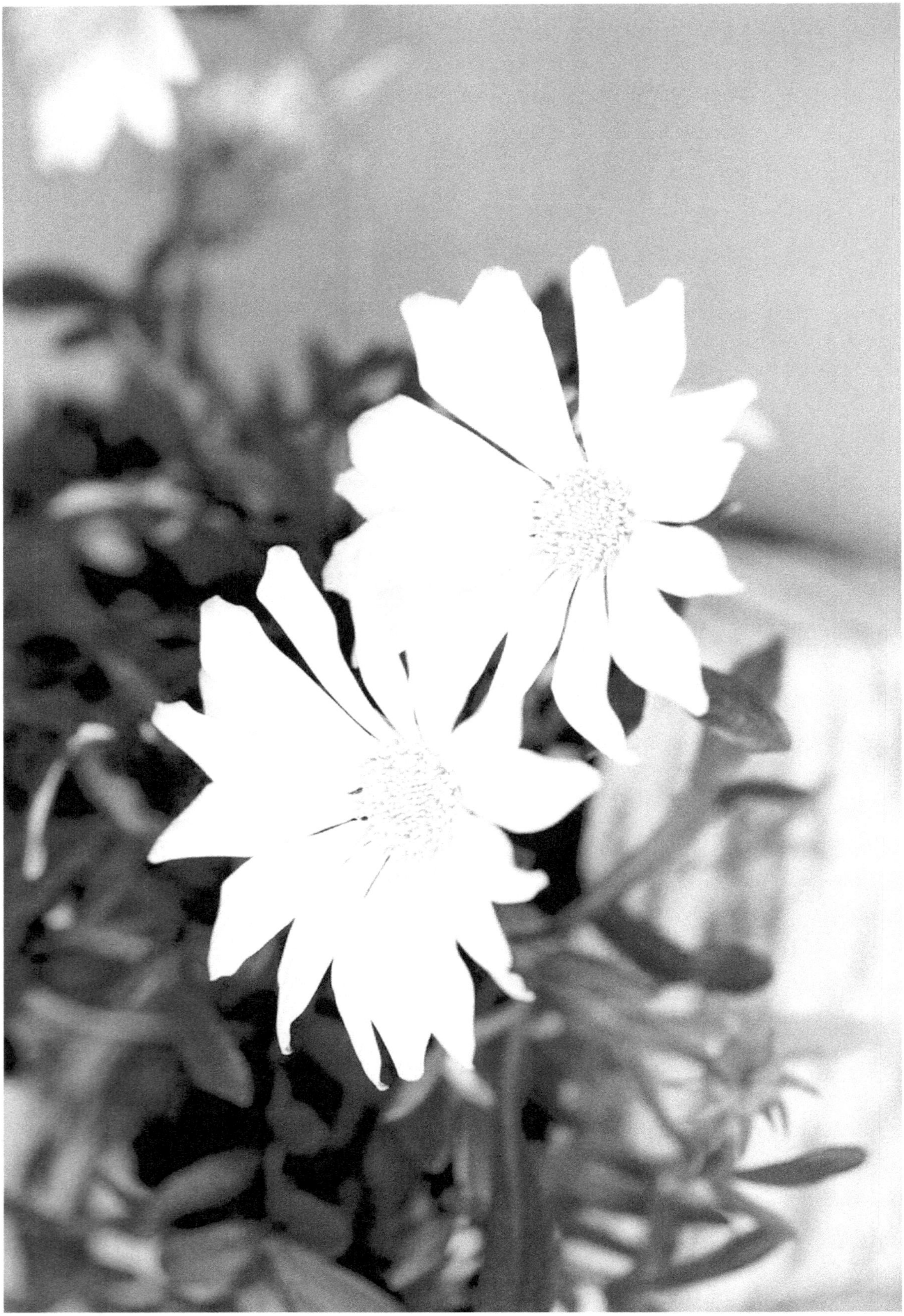

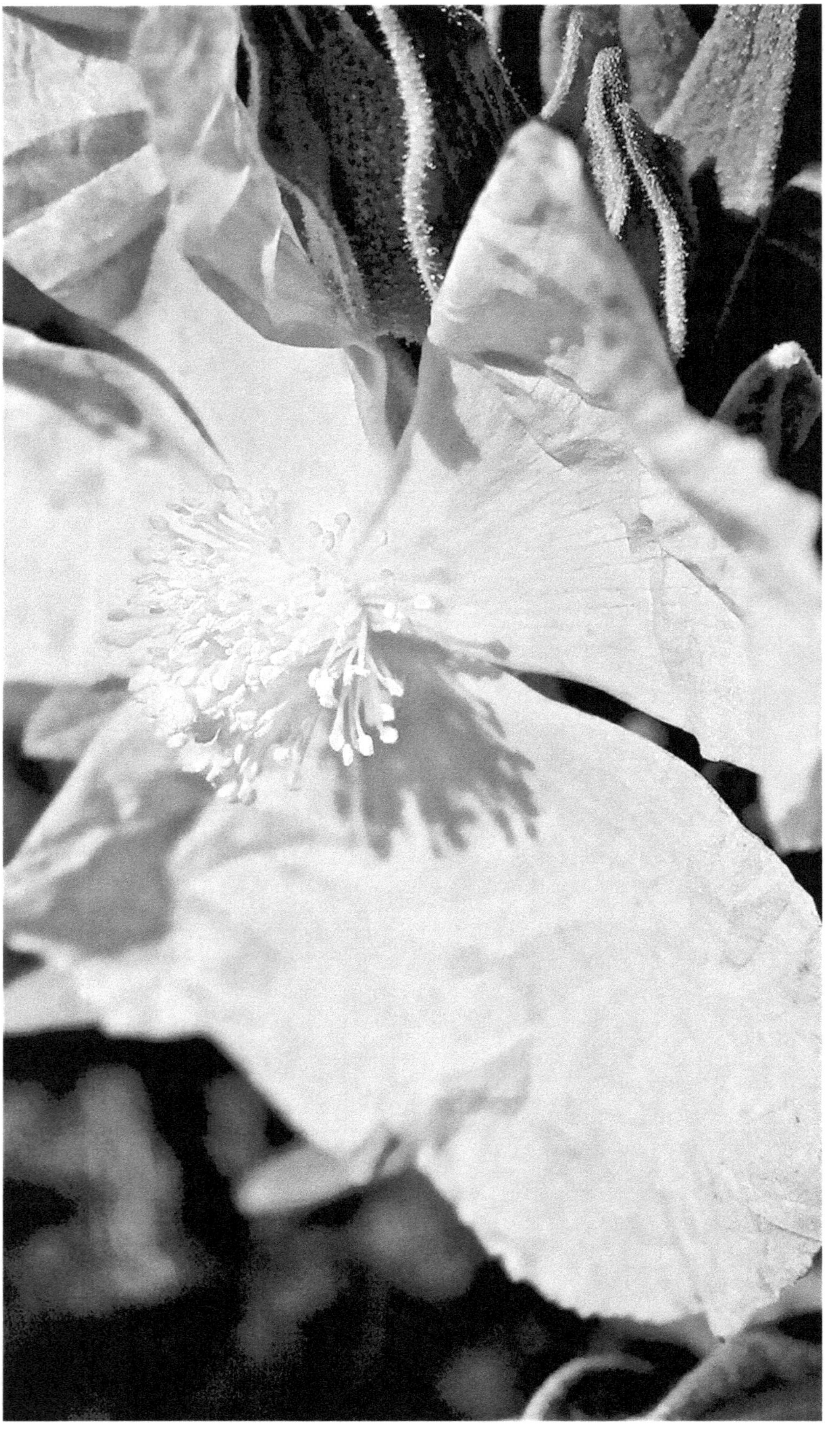

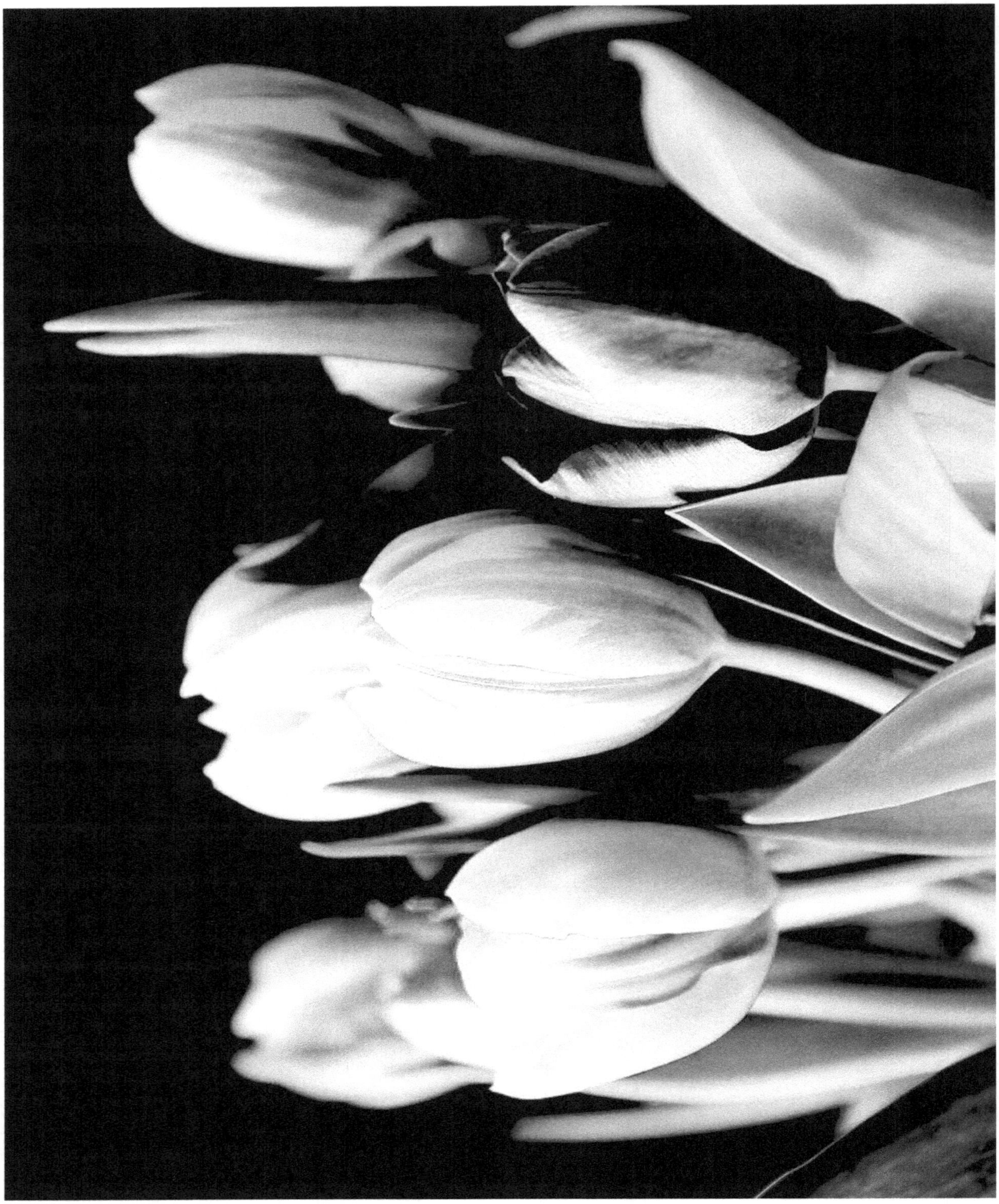

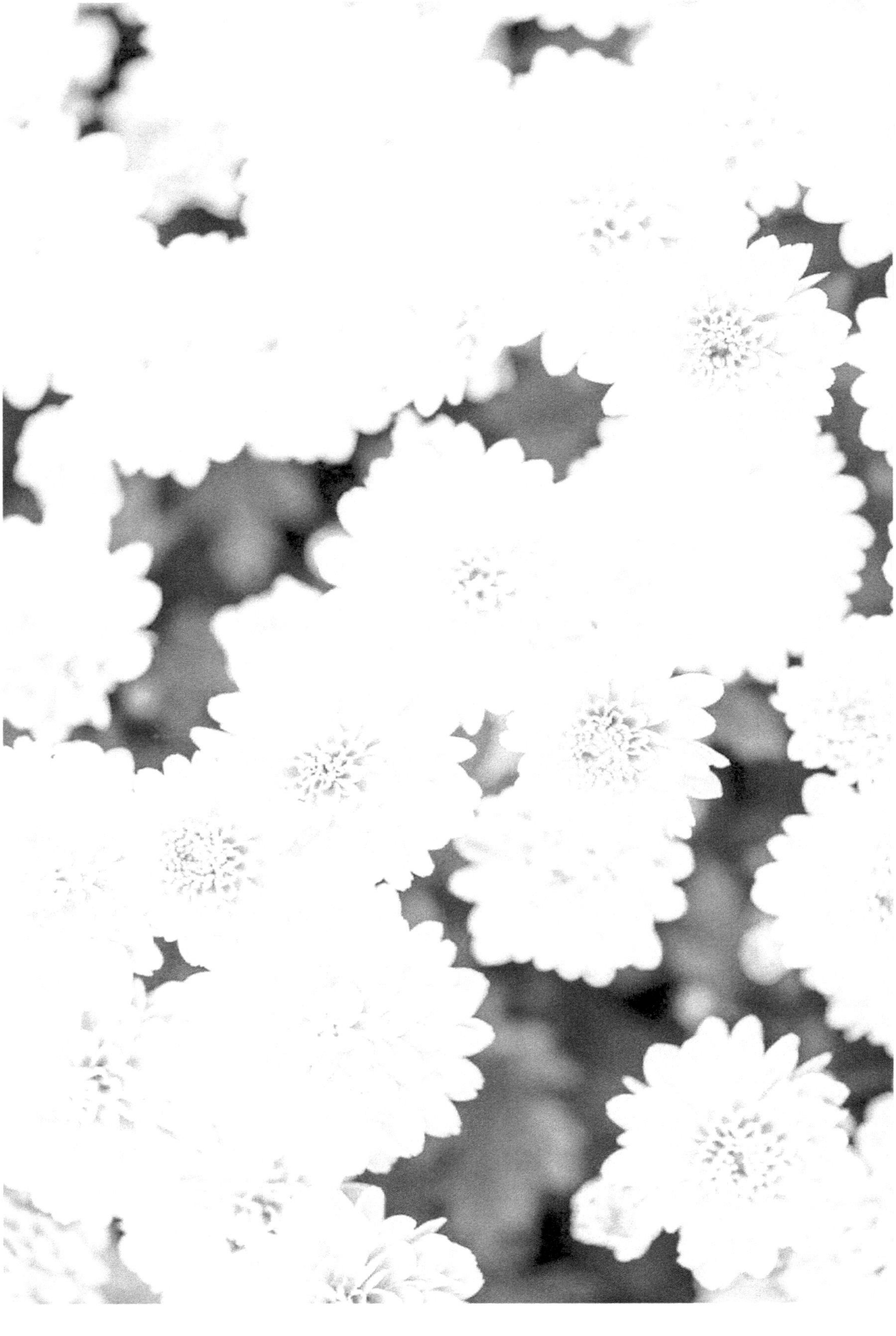

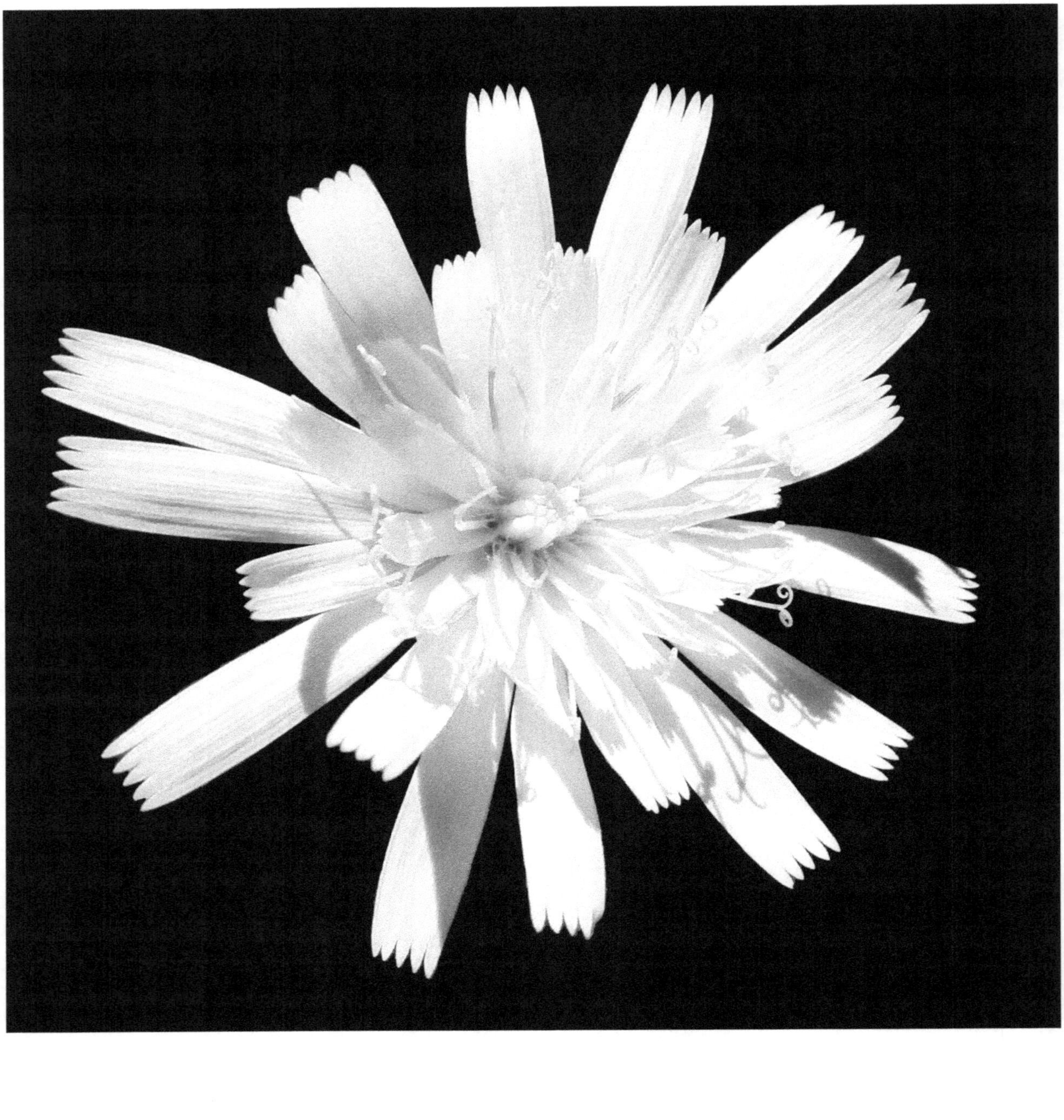

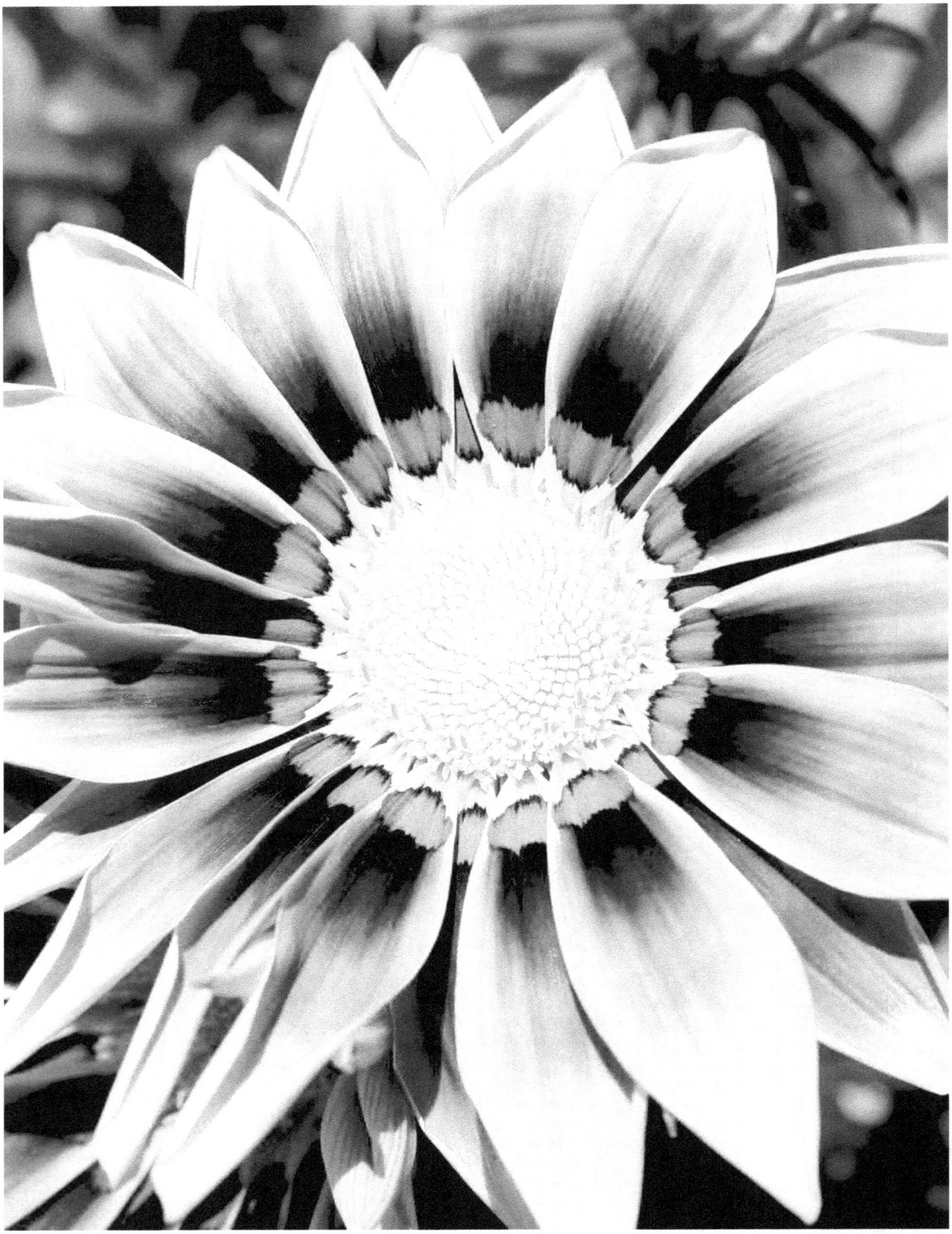

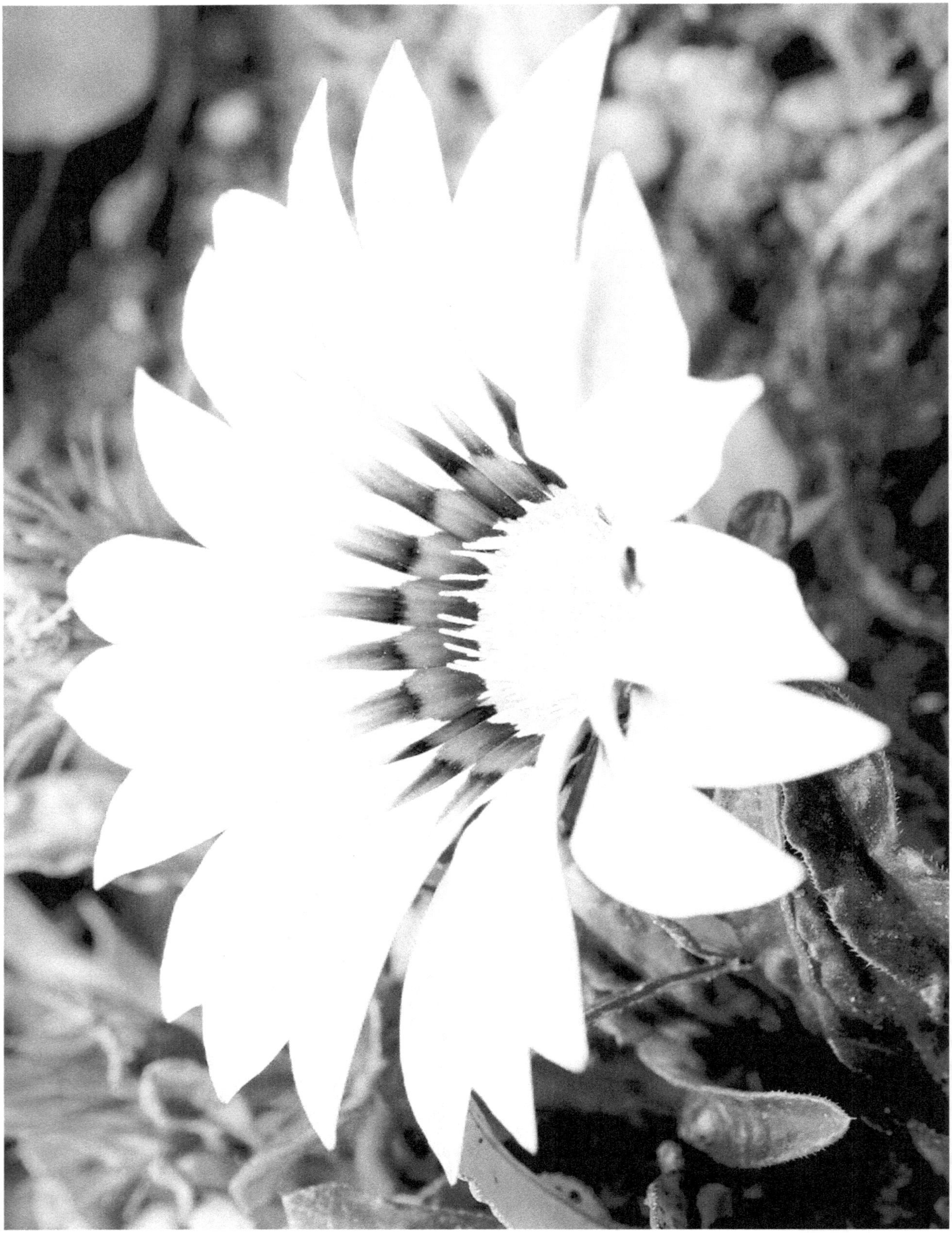

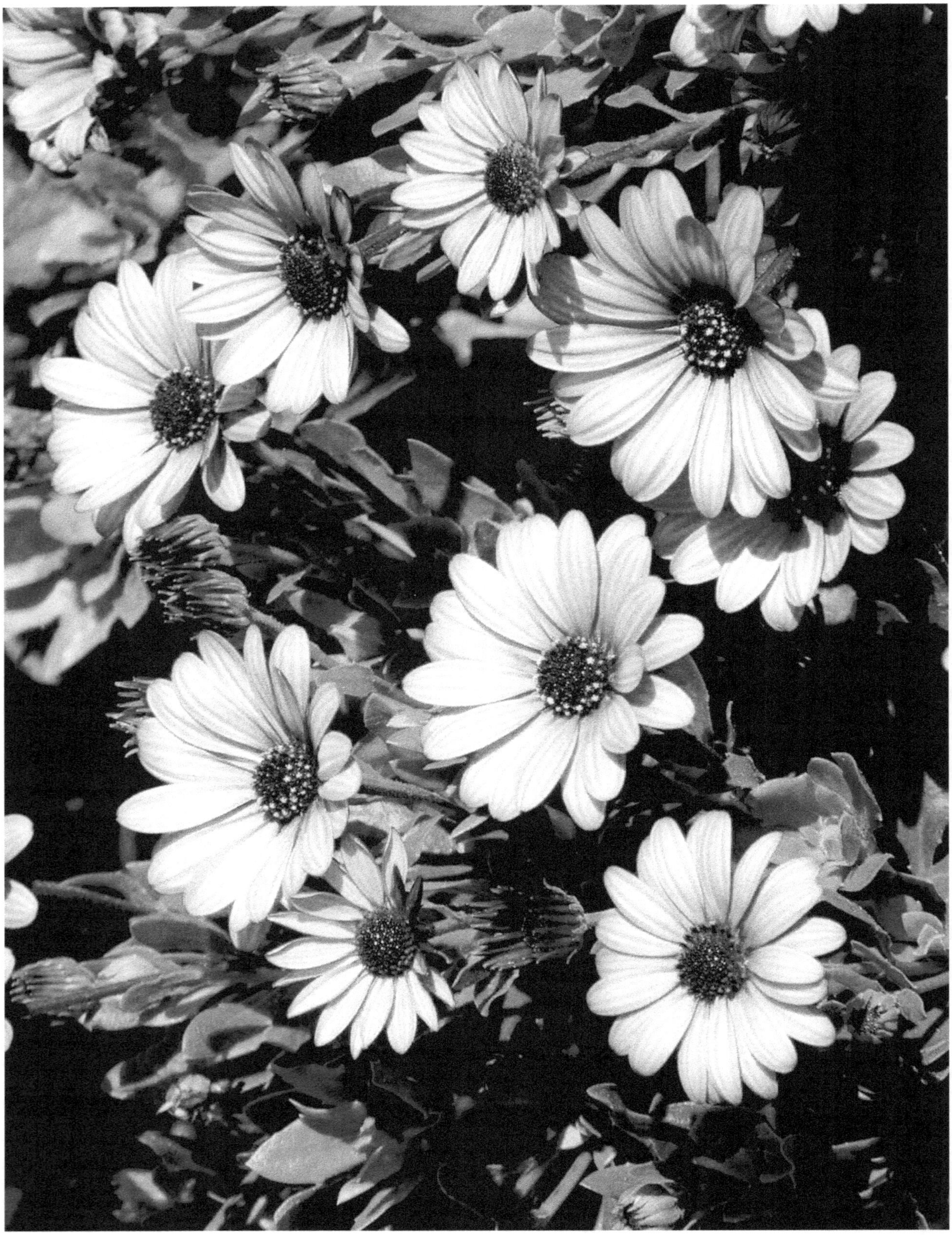

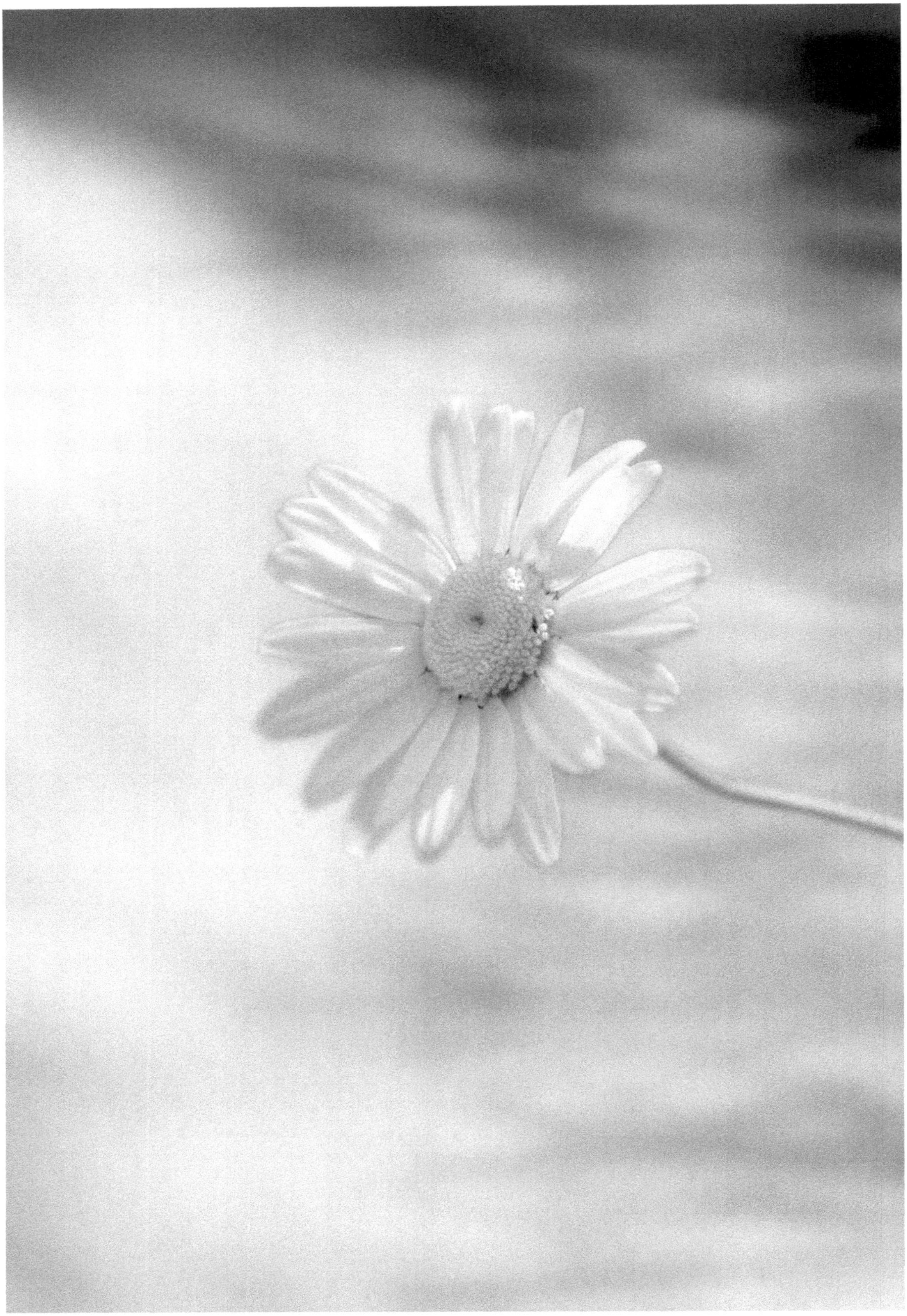

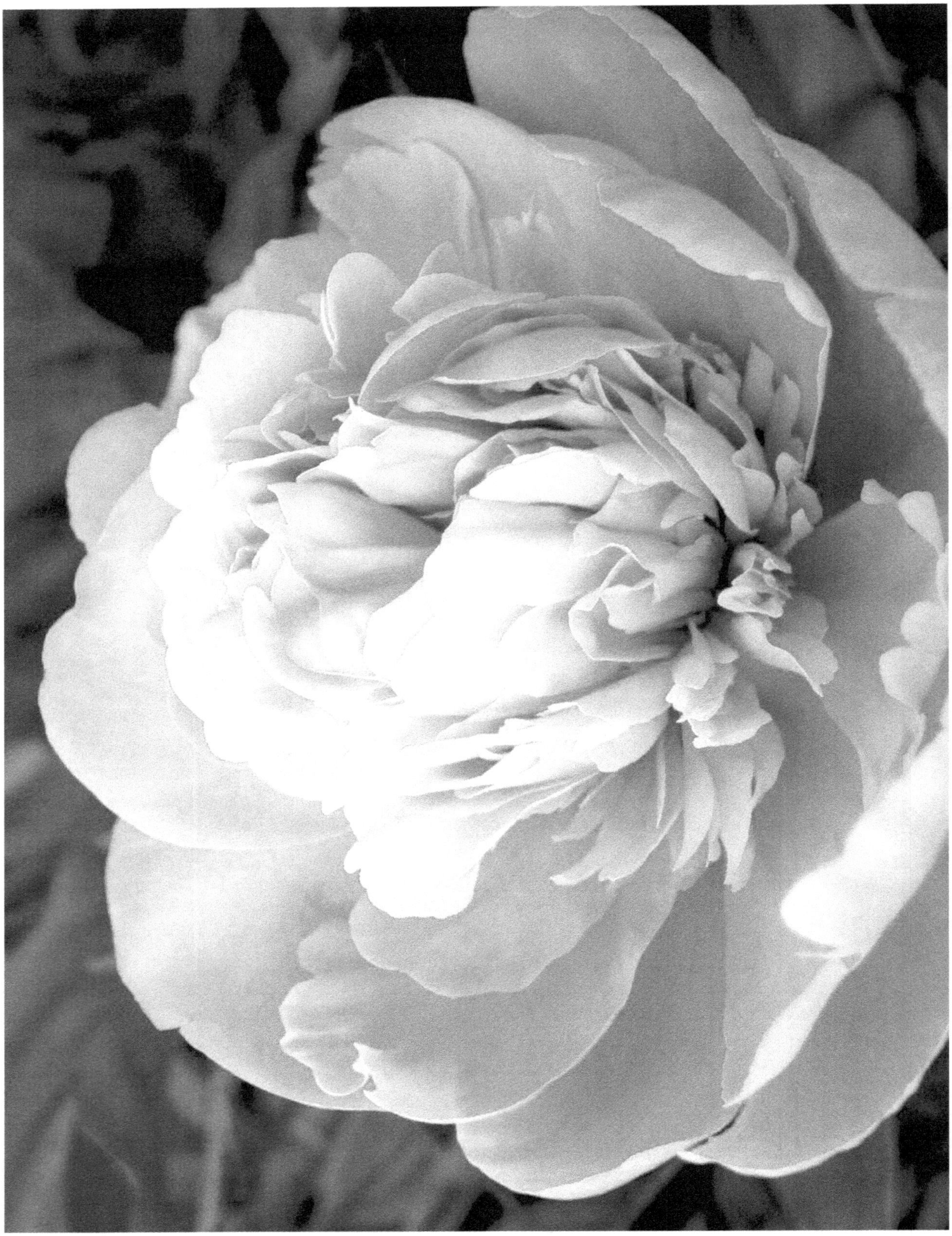

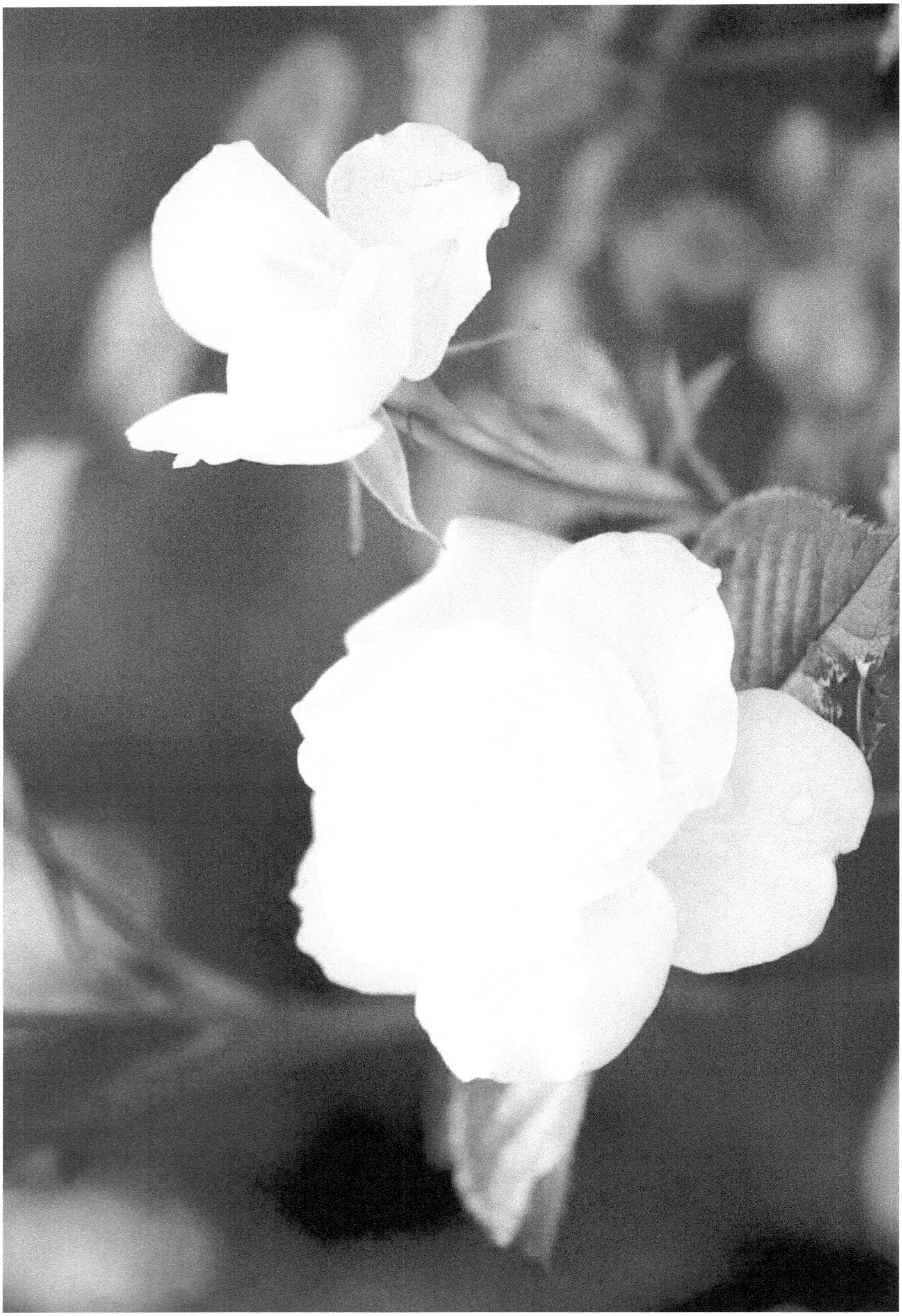

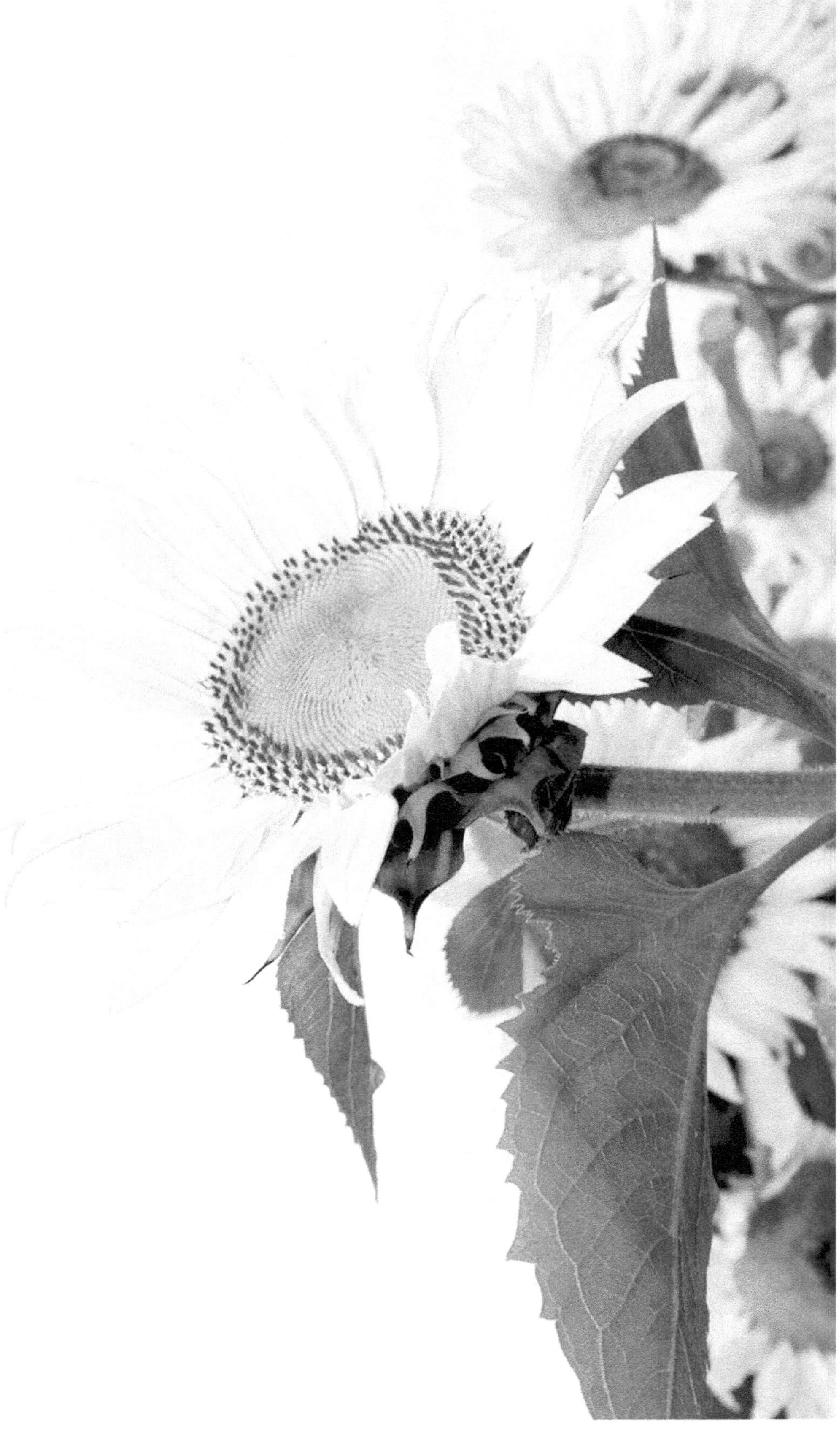

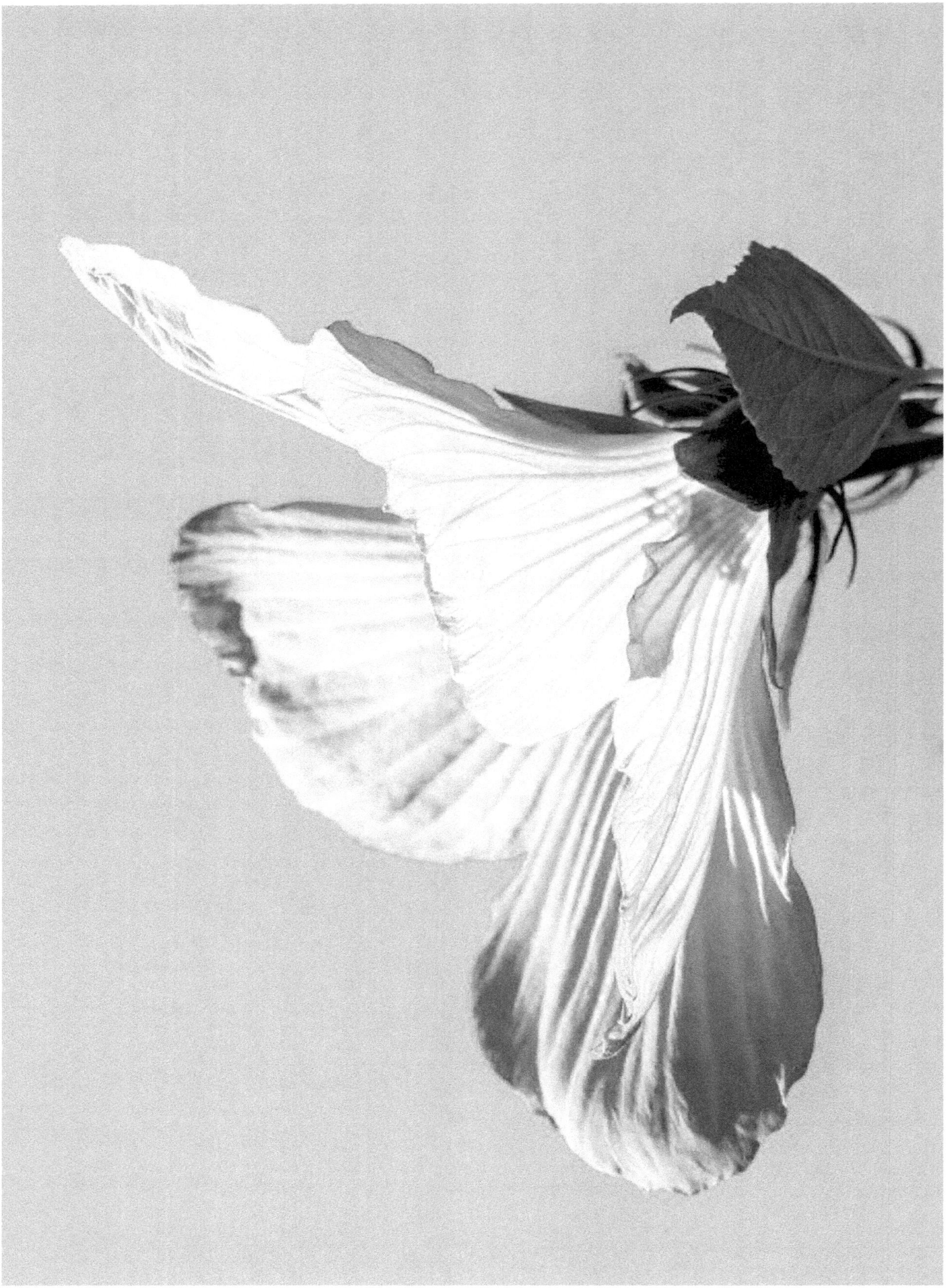

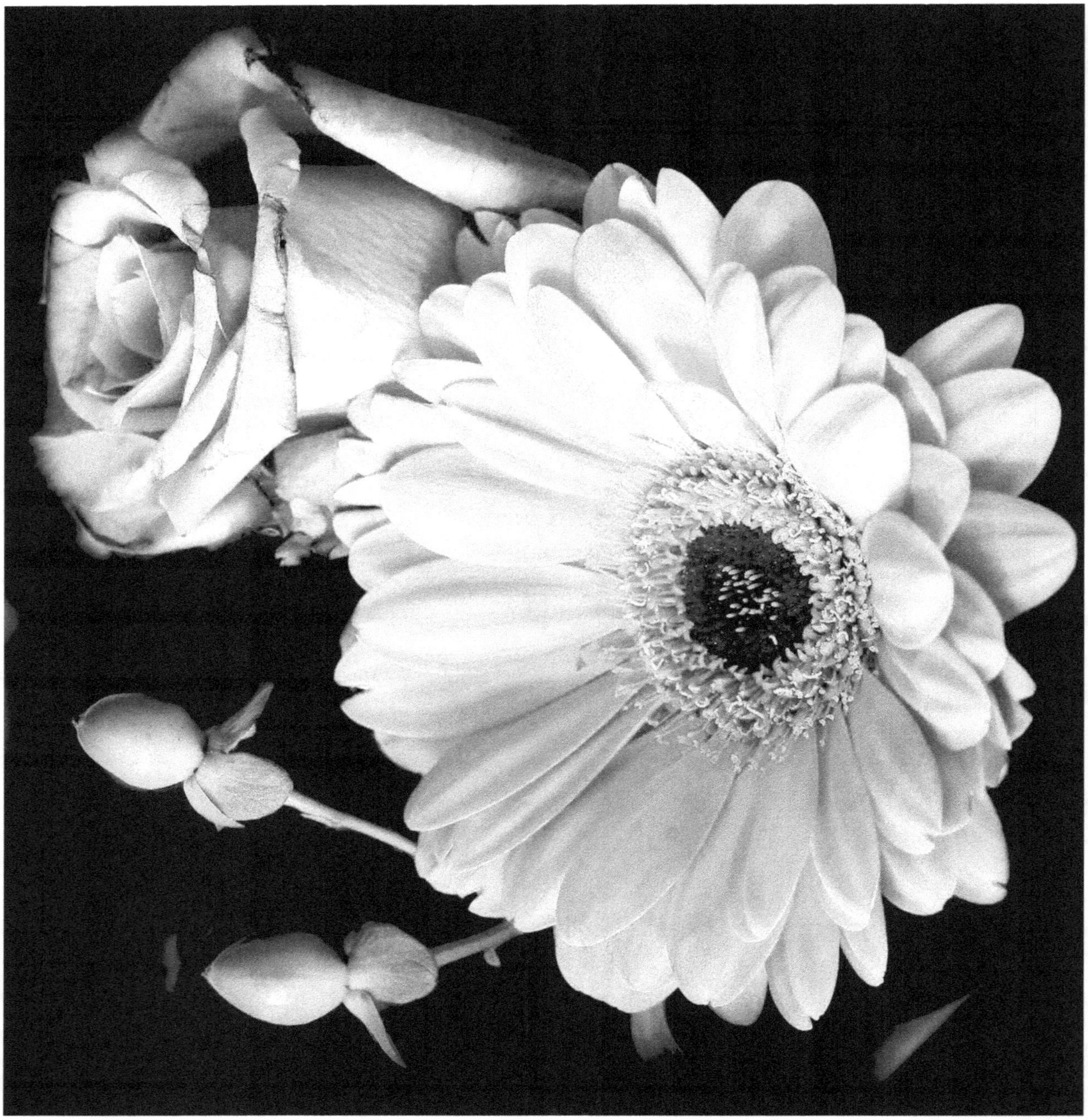

www.ingramcontent.com/pod-product-compliance
Lightning Source LLC
Chambersburg PA
CBHW080553190526
45169CB00007B/2758
9781537077291